Stocking Stuffer

CRAFTS

Publications International, Ltd.

CONTRIBUTING CRAFT DESIGNERS:
Lori Blankenship (pages 31, 34), Christine DeJulio (pages 27, 38, 40), Suzann Thompson (pages 10, 24, 44), Maria Nerius (pages 17, 46), Kathleen Marie O'Donnell (pages 12, 29, 52), Judith Sandstrom (pages 19, 50, 54, 61), Carol L. Neu (pages 14, 42, 48, 59), Ricë Freeman-Zachery (pages 22, 36, 57)

TECHNICAL ADVISOR: Christine DeJulio
HAND MODEL: Theresa Lesniak/Royal Model Management
PHOTOGRAPHY: Sacco Productions Limited/Chicago
PHOTOGRAPHERS: Marc A. Frisco, Guy Moeller
PHOTO STYLIST: Mary B. Valentine
PRODUCTION: Paula M. Walters

SOURCE OF MATERIALS
Most products used in this book are available at your local arts and crafts stores. The following products were used in this book: **Page 10:** Kaleidoscope kit (Homecrafters Manufacturing Corp.); Celestial rub-on decals (Plaid Enterprises, Inc.); Gold beading paint (Tulip Productions). **Page 12:** Embroidery floss (The DMC Corp.); Plastic canvas (Darice, Inc.). **Page 14:** Mini wooden birdhouses (Walnut Hollow Farm, Inc.); Americana acrylic paints (DecoArt). **Page 17:** Ceramcoat acrylic paint (Delta Technical Coating, Inc.); Snowman wood cutout (Woodworks). **Page 22:** Alphabet stamp set (Stampa Barbara); Handprint stamp (Emerald City Stamps). **Page 24:** Facet beads, pendants, bicone beads, and flower spacers (The Beadery); Waxed linen cord (Darice, Inc.). **Page 29:** Embroidery floss (The DMC Corp.); Porcelain box (Anne Brinkley Designs, Inc.); Cross-Stitch fabric (Wichelt Imports, Inc.). **Page 31:** Brass charms (Creative Beginnings from the Cotton Ball). **Page 34:** Stickers (American Greetings); Prism acrylic paint (Palmer Paint Products, Inc.). **Page 36:** CraftStor Create-a-Caddy pencil holder (Eagle); Alphabet stamp set (Stampa Barbara); Crayon stamp (Rubber Stampede). **Page 40:** Totebag (Bagworks, Inc.); Illinois Bronze webbing spray (Sherwin-Williams Co.); Fabric paint (Plaid Enterprises, Inc.). **Page 42:** Wood disk (Cabin Craft Southwest, Inc.); Americana acrylic paints (DecoArt). **Page 44:** Bracelet memory wire (Gick Crafts); Letter and heart beads (Darice, Inc.). **Page 46:** Muslin bag (Bagworks, Inc.); Wood cutouts (Woodworks); Ceramcoat acrylic paints (Delta Technical Coatings, Inc.); Dimensional fabric paint (Tulip Productions). **Page 48:** Metallic paints (DecoArt); Photo album (Dalee Book Co.). **Page 50:** HeatnBond iron-on flexible vinyl (Therm O Web, Inc.). **Page 52:** Embroidery floss (The DMC Corp.); Plastic canvas (Darice, Inc.). **Page 57:** Indian corn stamp (Stampa Barbara); Lettuce, green beans, carrots, and radishes stamps (100 Proof Press). **Page 59:** Wood and wire hanging sign kit (Walnut Hollow Farm, Inc.); Americana acrylic paints (DecoArt); FolkArt acrylic paints (Plaid Enterprises, Inc.).

Contents

Introduction

Bring Christmas cheer to all with *Stocking Stuffer Crafts*. You'll find everything from cross-stitch to jewelry. Now you'll be able to make something wonderful for everyone on your gift list—and each project can be made in less than a day!

What You'll Find
Jewelry Making

Although the jewelry in this book looks sophisticated, most are made by gluing. Jewelry findings is a term for a variety of ready-made metal components used as attachments and fastenings to assemble a piece of jewelry. They are usually made of inexpensive metal. Findings include pin backs, earring findings, barrel clasps, jump rings, and beading wire. All of these items are easily found in your local craft or hobby store.

Polymer Clay

There are several polymer clays on the market. All are intermixable and offer you endless options for creating different objects. The clays are quite hard when first unwrapped and must be kneaded until soft and pliable. Make sure not to use the clay before it reaches this stage—if you do, you may create air pockets and cracks when you roll it out. This can cause the clay to break apart. After you have worked your clay until it is soft, roll it into logs. You can proceed with your project at this point.

When you have finished forming your clay object, you will need to bake it to harden it. Follow instructions on package for baking times and temperatures.

Cross-Stitch

Fabric: Cross-stitch is traditionally worked on an "even-weave" cloth that has vertical and horizontal threads of equal thickness and spacing. The most common even-weave fabric is 14-count Aida cloth. The weave of this fabric creates distinct squares that make stitching very easy for the beginner.

Needles, Hoops, and Scissors: A blunt-end or tapestry needle is used for counted cross-stitch. A #24 needle is the recommended size for stitching on 14-count Aida cloth. You may use an embroidery hoop while stitching—just be sure to remove it when not working on your project. A small pair of sharp scissors is a definite help when working with embroidery floss.

Floss: Six-strand cotton embroidery floss is most commonly used, and it's usually cut into 18-inch lengths for stitching. Use two of the six strands for stitching on 14-count Aida cloth.

Preparing to Stitch

The patterns in this book will tell you what size the overall stitched area will be when completed. It will also tell you what size piece of cloth to use.

To locate the center of the design, lightly fold your fabric in half and in half again to form quarters. Find the center of the chart by following the arrows on the sides.

Reading the chart is easy, since each square on the chart equals one stitch on the fabric. The colors correspond to the floss numbers listed in the color key. Select a color and stitch all of that color within an area. Begin by holding the thread ends behind the fabric until secured or covered over with two or three stitches. You may skip a few stitches on the back of the material, but do not run the thread from one area to another behind a section that will not be stitched in the finished piece—it will show through the fabric. If your thread begins to twist, drop the needle and allow the thread to untwist. It is important to the final appearance of the project to keep an even tension when pulling stitches through so that all stitches will have a uniform look. To end a thread, weave or run the thread under several stitches on the back side. Cut the ends close to the fabric.

Each counted cross-stitch is represented by a colored square on the project's chart. For horizontal rows, work the stitches in two steps, i.e., all of the left to right stitches and then all of the right to left stitches (see Figure A). For vertical rows, work each complete stitch as shown in Figure B.

FIGURE A
CROSS-STITCH

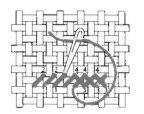

FIGURE B
VERTICAL CROSS-STITCH

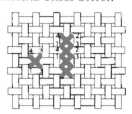

Plastic Canvas

Plastic Canvas: Canvas is most widely available by the sheet. Stitch all the pieces of a project on the same brand of plastic canvas to ensure that the meshes will match when you join them together.

Plastic canvas comes in several counts or mesh sizes (number of stitches to the inch) and numerous sizes of sheets. Specialty sizes and shapes such as circles are also available. Most canvas is clear, although up to 24 colors are available. Designs can be stitched on any mesh count—the resulting size of the project is the only thing that will be affected. The smaller the count number, the larger the project will be, since the count number refers to the number of stitches per inch. Therefore, 7-count has seven stitches per inch, while 14-count has 14 stitches per inch. A 14-count project will be half the size of a 7-count project if identical projects were stitched on 7-count and 14-count canvas.

Needles: Needle size is determined by the count size of the plastic canvas you are using. Patterns generally call for a #18 needle for stitching on 7-count plastic canvas, a #16 or #18 for 10-count canvas, and a #22 or #24 for stitching on 14-count plastic canvas.

Yarns and Embroidery Floss: While a wide variety of yarns may be used, the projects in this book use embroidery floss. Sport weight yarn (or 3-ply) and embroidery floss are often used on 10-count canvas. Use 12 strands or double the floss thickness for 10-count canvas, and use 6 strands for stitching on 14-count canvas.

Cutting Out Your Project
Many plastic canvas projects are dimensional—a shape has to be cut out and stitched. Scissors or a craft knife are recommended.

Preparing to Stitch
Cut your yarn or embroidery floss to a 36-inch length. Begin by holding the yarn end behind the canvas until secured or covered over with two or three stitches. To end a length, weave or run the yarn under several stitches on the back side. Cut the end close to the canvas. The continental stitch is the most commonly used stitch to cover plastic canvas. Decorative stitches will add interest and texture to your project. As in cross-stitch, if your yarn begins to twist, drop the needle and allow the yarn to untwist. It is important to the final appearance of the project to keep an even tension when pulling your stitches through so that all of your stitches have a uniform look. Do not pull your stitches too tight, since this causes gaps in your stitching and allows the canvas to show through between your stitches. Also, do not carry one color yarn across too many rows of another color on the back—the carried color may show through to the front of your project. Do not stitch the outer edge of the canvas until the other stitching is complete. If the project is a single piece of canvas, overcast the outer edge with the color specified. If there are two or more pieces, follow the pattern instructions for assembly. The following stitches are used in plastic canvas.

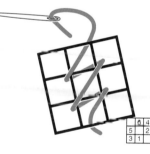

Mosaic Stitch
For the mosaic stitch, your needle comes up at 1 and all odd-numbered holes and goes down at 2 and all even numbered holes.

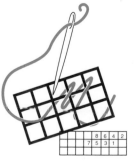

Continental Stitch
For the continental stitch, your needle comes up at 1 and all odd-numbered holes and goes down at 2 and all even-numbered holes.

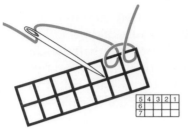

Overcast Stitch
For the overcast stitch, the needle goes down at the numbered holes, and the yarn wraps over the edge of the canvas. Make sure to cover the canvas completely.

Sewing

Scissors: Two styles are needed, one about eight to ten inches long with a bent handle for cutting fabric. These shears should be sharp and used only for fabric. The second style of scissors is smaller, about six inches, with sharp points. You will need this style for smaller projects and close areas.

Straight Pins: Nonrusting dressmaker's pins are best to use. They will not leave rust marks on your fabric if they come in contact with dampness or glue. And dressmaker's pins have very sharp points for easy insertion.

Tape Measure: Should be plastic coated so that it will not stretch and can be wiped off if it comes in contact with paint or glue.

Ironing Board and Steam Iron: Be sure your ironing board is well padded and has a clean covering. Sometimes you do more sewing with the iron than you do with the sewing machine. A steam or dry iron is best. It is important to press your fabric to achieve a professional look. The iron is also used to adhere the fusible webbing. Keep the bottom of your iron clean and free of any substance that could mark your fabric. The steam iron may be used directly on most fabrics with no shine. Test a small piece of the fabric first. If it causes a shine on the right side, try the reverse side.

Thread: Have mercerized sewing thread in the colors needed for each project you have chosen. Proper shade and strength (about a 50 weight) of thread avoids having the stitching show more than is necessary, and the item will have a finished look.

Fusible Webbing (or adhesive): The webbing is placed paper side up on wrong side of material. Place iron on paper side of adhesive and press for one to three seconds. Allow fabric to cool. Design can then be drawn or traced onto the paper side and cut out. Remove the paper and place the material right side up in desired position on project and iron for three to five seconds.

Sewing Machine: Neat, even stitches are achieved in very few minutes with a sewing machine, and it helps you complete your project with ease.

Work Surface: Your sewing surface should be a comfortable height for sitting and roomy enough to lay out your projects. Keep it clean and free of other crafting materials that could accidently spill on or soil your fabric.

Fabric Painting

Paints: Only dimensional and embellished paints, which are especially formulated to use on fabric, are used. For specific instructions for each paint, follow the instructions on the packaging or bottle.

Basic Guidelines for Fabric Painting

1. If you're right-handed, work on your project from the upper left-hand corner to the lower right-hand corner. Paint all colors as you go. This will prevent you from accidentally smearing the paint with your elbow or hand.

2. When using dimensional paints, pick up the tube of paint with the cap on and shake the paint down into the tip to remove any air bubbles each time you use a color. Place a paint bottle down on its side between uses.

3. Hold your dimensional paint bottle like a ball-point pen. Squeeze gently to push out paint. Work quickly and smoothly. Moving too slowly often results in a "bumpy" appearance.

4. Allow paints to dry at least 6 to 8 hours before touching. Allow 36 to 48 hours for paint to be completely cured before wearing.

Tie-Dye

Tie-dye is a fabulous craft for children as well as adults. However, it is not a craft that children should do on their own. It requires adult supervision! Keep the following information in mind when you plan to tie-dye with children.

• The work area should be protected from accidental spills and splashes. Use plastic, possibly covered with newspapers or old towels for absorbency.

• Have the children wear old clothes.

- An adult should always mix the dyes. Some dyes can be harmful in their unmixed form. Most should also be mixed with hot water. Read the package instructions carefully.

- Wear rubber gloves and make the children wear rubber gloves.

Dyes

There are several different fabric dyes. Some powdered and liquid dyes can be found in department stores or craft stores. Professional dyes, which will give the brightest colors, can be bought at art supply stores.

Ties

Rubber bands are most often used for tying the fabric before dyeing. Other methods involve tying knots in the fabric or tightly wrapping cording or string around different areas. Whatever method you are using, make sure the fabric is wrapped as tightly as possible. If it is not wrapped tightly, the dye will seep under your tie.

Methods for Dyeing

The easiest way to dye is by immersing projects in a bucket of dye. This is called a dye bath or tub dyeing. Be sure the item can move freely in the dye. Stir the project often so that the dye gets to all areas of the garment.

Using squeeze bottles or a paint brush to apply dye to specific areas will give you more control. You can buy squeeze bottles, or old (cleaned) dishwashing detergent bottles can be used.

Tips for Success

Always wash your garment to remove any dirt and sizing. Do not use fabric softeners or dryer sheets when prewashing your garments.

The length of time you leave the dye on your garment will also determine how deep your colors will be. Use the times we have given to get results similar to ours. Also, choose 100 percent cotton fabrics or other all natural fibers (like linen, silk, or wool). These will give you the truest colors.

Rinsing the item before removing the rubber bands keeps color off the tied areas. Rinse the project after dyeing with warm followed by cool water. Always read the manufacturer's instructions. If several colors are used, rinse one area at a time so that the colors don't run together. Letting the garment dry flat will keep the colors separate, too.

Decorative Wood Painting

Paints

There are a wide variety of paint brands to choose from. Acrylic paints are available at your local arts and crafts stores in a wide variety of brands. Acrylic paint dries in minutes and allows projects to be completed in no time at all. Clean hands and brushes with soap and water.

Finishes

Choose from a wide variety of types and brands of varnishes to protect your finished project. Varnish is available in spray and brush-on varieties.

Brush-on water-base varnishes dry in minutes and clean up with soap and water. Use over any acrylic paints only.

Spray varnishes can be used over any type of paint or medium. For projects with a pure white surface, choose a nonyellowing varnish. Varnishes are available in matte, satin, or gloss finishes. Choose the shine you prefer.

Brushes and Paint Supplies

Foam (sponge) brushes work great to seal, basecoat, and varnish wood. Clean brushes with soap and water when using acrylic paints and mediums.

Synthetic brushes work well with acrylic paints for details and designs. Use a liner brush for thin lines and details. A script brush is needed for extra long lines. Round brushes fill in round areas, stroke work, and broad lines. An angle brush is used to fill in large areas, float a shade, or side load color. A large flat brush is used to apply basecoat and varnish. Small flat brushes are for stroke work and basecoating small areas.

Wood Preparation

Properly preparing your wood piece can make all the difference in the outcome. Having a smooth surface to work on will allow you to complete the project quickly and easily. Once the wood is prepared, you are ready to proceed with a basecoat, stain, or finish, according to the project instructions.

Here are the supplies you will need to prepare the wood: sand paper (#200) for removing roughness; tack cloth, which is a sticky resin treated cheese cloth, to remove dust after sanding; a wood sealer to seal wood and prevent warping; and a foam or 1-inch flat brush to apply sealer.

Basic Painting Techniques

THIN LINES

1. Thin paint with 50 percent water for a fluid consistency that flows easily off the brush. It should be about ink consistency.

2. Use a liner brush for short lines and tiny details or a script brush for long lines. Dip brush into thinned paint. Wipe excess on palette.

3. Hold brush upright with handle pointing to the ceiling. Use your little finger as a balance when painting. Don't apply pressure for extra thin lines.

FLOATING COLOR

This technique is also called side loading. It is used to shade or highlight the edge of an object. Floated color is a gradual blend of color to water.

1. Moisten an angle brush with water. Blot excess water from brush, setting bristles on paper towel until shine of water disappears.

2. Dip the long corner of angle brush into paint. Load paint sparingly. Carefully stroke brush on palette until color blends halfway across the brush. If the paint blends all the way to the short side, clean

the brush and load it again. For thicker paint, dilute first with 50 percent water.

3. Hold the brush at a 45 degree angle, and using a light touch, apply color to designated area.

DOTS

Perfect round dots can be made with any round implement. The size of the implement determines the size of the dot. You can use the wooden end of a brush, a stylus tip, a pencil tip, or the eraser end of a pencil (with an unused eraser).

Use undiluted paint for thick dots or dilute paint with 50 percent water for smooth dots. Dip the tip into paint and then onto the surface. For uniform dots, you must redip in paint for each dot. For graduated dots, continue

dotting with same paint load. Clean tip on paper towel after each group and reload.

Rubber Stamps

Stamps

Look for two general styles of images: solid and line-art. A solid image lets you quickly get a lot of color onto a surface. Just a tap on an ink pad will do. A line-art image shows the outline and details of an image, rather than a solid mass. Once it's stamped, the impression is ready for hand coloring with pencils or markers.

Inks

Begin with ink pads that use standard, dye-based ink. These are water-based inks; never use permanent inks for the projects described in this book. Permanent inks will ruin your stamps. Dye-based inks are easy to use, and the ink dries quickly. This type of ink pad is sold everywhere and comes in dozens of colors.

Pigment ink is thick, opaque, and slow-drying—not good for slick surfaces, but perfect for embossing. Pigment ink also works well when stamping on polymer clay.

Papers

Begin with several types of white and light-colored matte papers with smooth surfaces. Try to get paper that doesn't bleed when you stamp it (unless you want a fuzzy effect).

You also need ordinary scrap paper. You'll use it to see how your stamps print, to test all your inks, to experiment with techniques, and to make preliminary designs for projects. And save old newspapers, too—you'll need them to protect your work area.

Tools

The right equipment can put you in stamper's paradise. As you gain experience, you should have as many of these items as possible: colored pencils, water-based brush markers, embossing powders and embossing gun, glitter glue, scissors, pinking shears, glue gun, craft knives and cutting mat, brayer, fabric ink and marking pens, eraser carving material and carving tools, stamp positioning tool, and cosmetic sponges.

Techniques

No matter which stamping project sparks your imagination, you need to understand the basics first. Keep these tips in mind:

1. The stamp, ink, and paper (or other medium) are most important, and each affects the other. Experiment every time you get a new stamp to see how it takes ink and leaves an impression. Check out its resiliency, and observe how it stamps on different papers or surfaces. Test new ink pads and papers as well.

2. Learn how to ink a stamp. Tap the stamp gently two or three times on a pad. Turn it over to see how well it's inked. Stamp it on scrap paper to get a feel for applying the right amount of ink to a die, or stamp. Too little ink causes details to be lost and colors to look pale, while too much obscures details. The image on a new die usually needs heavier inking because the fresh surface is so porous. Never pound or rock a die when inking.

3. Perfect your general stamping technique. Make a stamp impression by gently and evenly applying the inked die to the paper or other surface. Do not grind or rock the die (unless you're trying to achieve an unusual effect or are working with a curved surface).

4. Always work with clean stamps. Clean off each die before you switch from one color to another and after you're finished using it. Use warm water to moisten a paper towel, sponge, or small rag. Tap the stamp on the damp rag to remove ink.

5. Protect your stamps when they're not in use. Store them with the die side down, out of direct sunlight, and away from dust. Line your stamp storage container with thick construction paper.

A Word About Glue

There are many different glues on the craft market today, each formulated for a different crafting purpose. The following are used in this book:

White Glue: This may be used as an all-purpose glue—it dries clear and flexible. It is often referred to as craft glue or tacky glue. Tacky on contact, it allows you to put two items together without a lot of set up time required. Use for most projects, especially ones involving wood, plastics, some fabrics, and cardboard.

Hot Melt Glue: Formed into cylindrical sticks, this glue is inserted into a hot-temperature glue gun and heated to a liquid state. Depending on the type of glue gun used, the glue is forced out through the gun's nozzle by either pushing on the end of the glue stick or squeezing a trigger. Use clear glue sticks for projects using wood, fabrics, most plastics, ceramics, and cardboard. When using any glue gun, be careful of the nozzle and the freshly applied glue—it is very hot! Apply glue to the piece being attached. Work with small areas at a time so the glue doesn't set before being pressed into place.

Celestial Kaleidoscope

Vibrant beads, shimmering charms, and textured ribbons create the beautiful views in this kaleidoscope. Be creative, and pick a variety of items in different colors to go in your handmade kaleidoscope.

What You'll Need

Kaleidoscope kit
3 crystal stars, 25mm
3 moon charms, 25mm
8 acrylic stars, 14mm
1 dark blue round bead, 10mm
1 inch rickrack, ¼-inch wide
1½ inches lace, 1-inch wide
1 navy blue foam sheet
8–10 celestial rub-on decals
Antique gold beading paint
1 yard rainbow-colored satin
ribbon, ⅜-inch wide
1 yard navy satin ribbon,
⅜-inch wide
All-purpose glue
Craft stick
Waxed paper
Emery board
Stylus

2. Using the pattern provided in the kit, cut foam sheet to the correct size for the kaleidoscope tube. Place foam piece in tube to test for fit. Remove foam and trim so ends do not overlap in the tube. Once fitted, remove foam from tube. Lay foam flat and use a craft stick to rub decals on foam piece (see photo for placement).

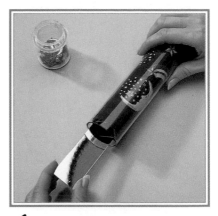

4. Use the emery board to round off the sharp edges of the plastic mirror pieces from the kaleidoscope kit. Remove protective film from mirrors. Place mirrors in the tube following kit instructions. When inserting the third mirror, run it down the seam of the foam very slowly and carefully. The fit is tight, but it will go in. The foam will hold the mirrors in their proper position.

5. Connect the tube and the viewing can from step 1 together to check for fit. Remove viewing can from tube, place glue around the plastic ring, and connect the viewing can back to the tube.

6. Using stylus, dot dabs of antique gold beading paint evenly spaced around the end of the tube near the eyepiece. Let paint dry. Glue rainbow ribbon around the viewing can above the plastic ring. Glue navy ribbon around the viewing can below the plastic ring. Tie each ribbon into a bow. Trim ends. Add dab of glue to knots to hold bows in place.

1. Glue 2 large crystal stars together back to back using craft glue. Glue 4 pairs of 14mm acrylic stars back to back. Place large stars, 4 pairs of 14mm stars, 3 moon charms, rickrack piece, lace piece, and blue round bead in the kaleidoscope viewing can. Place the plastic fitted ring from kaleidoscope kit on the viewing can. Set aside.

3. Cut a piece of waxed paper larger than the foam piece. Place waxed paper over decal side of foam. With decal side facing out, roll foam and waxed paper together to fit into tube. Be careful not to displace or wrinkle decals. Insert the roll all the way into tube. Carefully remove waxed paper, leaving the foam behind in tube.

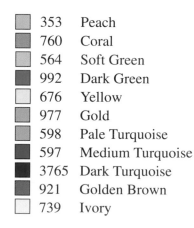

Navajo Dream Accessory Set

Subtle colors of the southwest accent

this charming purse accessory set.

A matching eyeglasses case and

checkbook cover will be gifts that are

used time and time again.

What You'll Need

2 sheets plastic canvas, 14 count
Ivory embroidery floss,
5 skeins for eyeglasses case and
8 skeins for checkbook cover
Embroidery floss, 1 skein each
(see color key below)
1 piece light brown felt,
6½ × 6½-inch for eyeglasses
case and 6½ × 12½-inch for
checkbook cover
#20 tapestry needle
Scissors
Craft glue

	353	Peach
	760	Coral
	564	Soft Green
	992	Dark Green
	676	Yellow
	977	Gold
	598	Pale Turquoise
	597	Medium Turquoise
	3765	Dark Turquoise
	921	Golden Brown
	739	Ivory

Eyeglasses Case

Cut 1 piece of plastic canvas 92×95-holes.

Stitching: Begin at the lower left corner of the shorter side (92 holes). Work 3 rows in continental stitch using ivory. Then stitch design following chart. Work design in continental stitch. After design is completed, work next 4 rows in continental stitch using ivory. Work the remainder of the piece in mosaic stitch using ivory.

To Finish: Glue 6½×6½-inch felt piece to back of stitched piece. Fold the eyeglass case in half with right side out. Overcast the top edges together using ivory. Repeat for left edges to form side seam.

Checkbook Cover

Cut 1 piece of plastic canvas 92×179-holes.

Background Stitching: Begin at the lower left corner of the shorter side (92 holes) and work 21 rows of mosaic stitch using ivory. (Note: The mosaic stitch uses 2 rows of plastic canvas. The 21 rows of mosaic stitch cover 42 rows of the plastic canvas.) Work continental stitch for the next 3 rows. When the 21 rows of mosaic stitch and 3 rows of continental stitch are complete, begin at the opposite end of plastic canvas and work 45 rows of mosaic stitch. Work continental stitch for the next 4 rows.

Design Stitching: Once background stitching is complete, work the design area following the chart. Work the design in continental stitch. Use the same background color to fill in around the design.

To Finish: Center and glue 6½×12½-inch felt piece to back of stitched piece. Fold checkbook cover as follows: Fold 1 end up at line between the 21 rows of mosaic stitches and 3 continental stitches. Fold other end up at line between rows 21 and 22 of mosaic stitch. Pin folds in place and overcast the raw edges together. Overcast remaining raw edges to finish.

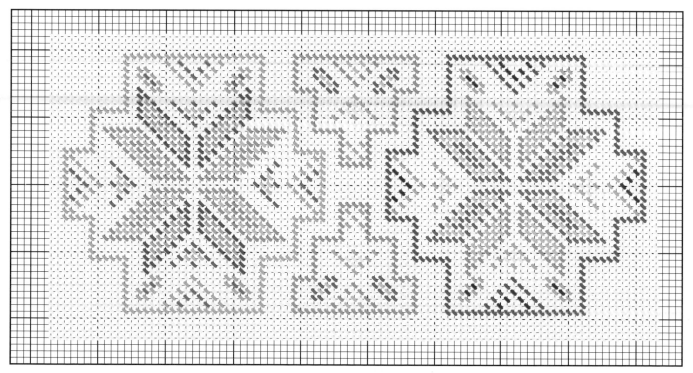

Enlarge at 140%

Birdhouse Plant Pokes

With Business Card Holder Variation

Are your plants just sitting there with no personality? Spruce up your greens with these little birdhouses, or convert one into a business card holder.

What You'll Need

(for each birdhouse)
Mini wood birdhouse
Wood dowel, ¼-inch diameter
Craft glue
Matte finish spray
Power drill, ¼-inch drill bit
Paintbrushes: ½-inch and #2 flat,
10/0 liner
Stylus *(for Diamond Birdhouse,
Cloud Home)*

Acrylic paints for:

Diamond Birdhouse:
buttermilk, french grey-blue,
uniform blue, avocado,
coral rose, light yellow

Birdie Barn:
cadmium red, snow white,
ebony black

Two-Story Home:
cashmere beige,
dark chocolate, cadmium red

Cloud Home:
buttermilk, colonial green,
teal green, avocado,
coral rose, ebony black

Wren Cottage:
buttermilk, colonial green,
teal green, avocado,
coral rose, ebony black

For business card holder add:
Small wood plaque
Plastic business card holder

Diamond Birdhouse
(with business card holder variation):

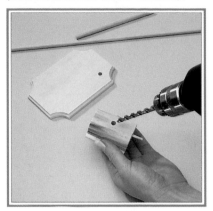

1. Cut wood dowel to 15 inches or desired length. For business card holder, cut wood dowel to 4 inches. Using the drill and ¼-inch drill bit, drill a hole into the business card holder plaque at one corner. Drill a ¼-inch hole in center bottom of mini wood birdhouse.

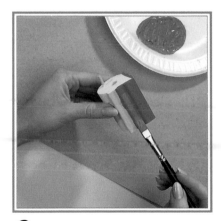

2. Use ½-inch flat brush to basecoat birdhouse walls and bottom with buttermilk. Let dry. Paint eaves and roof with french grey-blue. Use uniform blue to paint birdhouse perch and 15-inch dowel. Allow to dry. For business card holder, paint top and bottom of plaque french grey-blue and paint edges uniform blue.

3. Transfer diamond birdhouse pattern to front of birdhouse (see step 2 of Cook's Plaque on page 60). Line vine and leaves with avocado and let dry. Dot flowers with stylus using coral rose. Once paint is dry, dot flower centers with light yellow.

4. Add a dab of craft glue in drilled hole at bottom of birdhouse. Insert 15-inch dowel and let dry. For business card holder, apply a drop of craft gluc in both drilled holes (1 on birdhouse, 1 on plaque). Insert 4-inch dowel in hole on birdhouse. Insert other end of dowel in hole on plaque.

5. Spray with a matte finish. Let dry. For business card holder, use craft glue to secure card holder to plaque. Add optional trims, such as moss or a mini bird.

To make the other birdhouses, follow the same procedures described in steps 1 through 5 using appropriate paints and patterns. See finished project photo for paint placement.

Diamond Birdhouse

Front

WELCOME

Front

Wren Cottage

Side

Front

Cloud Home

Side

Birdie Barn

Front

Side

Two-Story Home

Front

Side

Nip in the Air Snowman Pin

Tuck a cozy snowman pin inside a special friend's stocking. It will help take away the chill of winter when it's pinned on a warm coat or heavy sweater.

What You'll Need

2-inch wood snowman cutout
Hand drill, 3/16-inch drill bit
Acrylic paints: white, black, cardinal red, pumpkin, copen blue
Toothpick
Scrap of red fabric
Bar pin, 1/2-inch long
Paintbrush
Stylus
Tacky glue
Hot glue gun and glue sticks
Wire cutter

1. Drill a small hole ¼-inch deep in center of snowman's face.

2. Basecoat body of snowman with white paint. Paint back and sides of body and be careful not to close up hole. Let dry. Basecoat front, back, and sides of hat with black paint. Allow to dry. Dot red cheeks and blue eyes on face with stylus. Dot 2 black buttons on body. Use black paint to dab 5 dots from cheek to cheek for smile on snowman's face.

3. Paint one end of toothpick with pumpkin. Cut ¼ inch off from end when dry. Dab a small amount of craft glue in hole on snowman's face. Insert cut end of toothpick in hole.

4. Glue scrap of red fabric around snowman's neck. Use hot glue to secure bar pin to back of snowman below scarf.

Golfer's Set

Give your favorite golf enthusiast this
three-piece ensemble for his or her next outing.
A pair of decorated boxer shorts, a stylish visor,
and a matching hand towel "fore" the golfer
make gifts that are way above "par."

What You'll Need

(for visor)
½ yard white fabric
5 inches fabric each: green, tan, red
½ yard iron-on fabric adhesive
¼ yard quilting fleece
15 inches green double-fold bias tape, ½-inch wide
10 inches white elastic, ¼-inch wide
Tracing or typing paper
Pencil
Iron
Scissors
Hole punch
Green thread
Sewing needle

(for boxer shorts and hand towel)
1 pair white boxer shorts
1 white hand towel
10 inches fabric each: green, tan, red, white
¼ yard iron-on fabric adhesive
Tracing or typing paper
Pencil
Iron
Scissors

Visor

1. Iron a 9×17-inch piece of fabric adhesive to back of white fabric. Trace 2 visors and golf ball pattern pieces on paper backing. Cut out 2 visor pieces and golf ball. Do not remove paper backings.

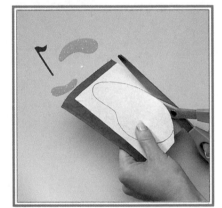

2. Iron small pieces of adhesive to back of green, tan, and red fabric pieces. Trace green on paper backing of green fabric, 2 sand traps on paper backing of tan fabric, and a flag on paper backing of red fabric. Cut out all pieces. Set pieces aside.

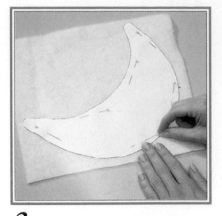

3. Pin paper visor pattern piece to quilting fleece. Cut a visor piece from fleece. Remove pins and pattern. Remove paper backing from second fabric visor piece. Place over fleece visor, lining up the edges. Press with iron to fuse pieces together.

4. Remove paper backing from first fabric visor piece. Place the 2 visor sections back to back with edges even. Press with iron to fuse sections together. Trim excess fleece around the edges.

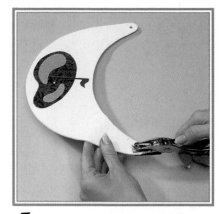

5. Remove paper backing from each applique piece and golf ball. Center green applique on front of visor and iron in place. Arrange sand traps, flag, and golf ball on green. Iron in place. Punch a hole at each end of visor ¼ inch from edge.

6. Using green thread and sewing needle, securely stitch each end of 10-inch elastic piece to inside of green bias tape 2 inches from each end. Stitch folded edges of the bias tape together, forming a casing. Pull ends of casing up through punched holes of visor and knot securely. Trim ends.

Boxer Shorts & Hand Towel

1. Iron adhesive to back of green, tan, red, and white fabric pieces. Trace 2 greens on paper backing of green fabric, 4 sand traps on paper backing of tan fabric, 2 flags on paper backing of red fabric, and 2 golf balls on paper backing of white fabric. Cut out pieces and remove paper backing from each applique.

2. For the boxer shorts, arrange applique pieces on the left side of the front 2 inches from the bottom. Press into place with iron. For the towel, center applique pieces 6 inches from each side and 3 inches from the bottom. Iron in place.

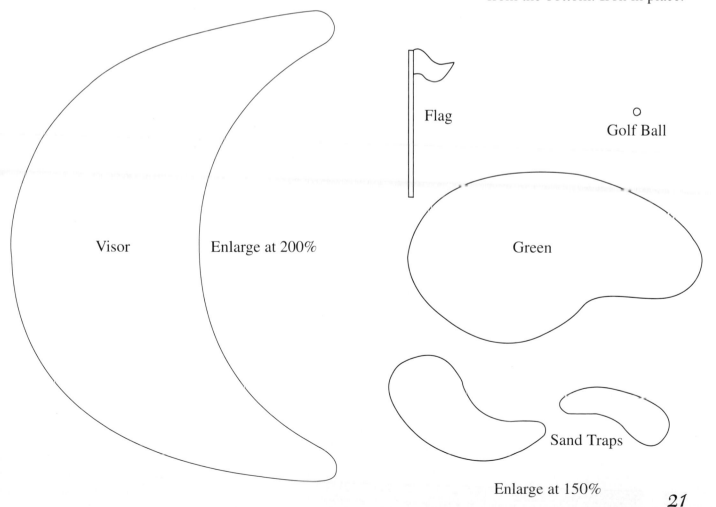

Flag

Golf Ball

Visor Enlarge at 200%

Green

Sand Traps

Enlarge at 150%

Coupon Book

Coupon books are popular gifts because they can easily be personalized. Your child can make one for mom, dad, grandma, or grandpa with a little help. It will melt the heart of any recipient. The hard part will be getting them to redeem the coupons!

What You'll Need

6–10 pieces white cardstock, 4×5-inches
Alphabet stamp set
Handprint stamp
Ink pads: yellow, blue, green, red
Crayons: yellow, blue, green, red
Sewing machine
Ruler
Hole punch
Rubber band

1.

3.

4.

1. Do not thread sewing machine. With adult help, run needle through 1 piece of cardstock ¾-inch from one edge to create perforated pages of coupon book. Repeat with remaining cards.

2. Pick out the alphabet stamps you need to spell out COUPON BOOK for MOM for the cover and GOOD FOR for the inside pages. Use all cardstock pieces except 1 for inside coupon book pages. Begin by inking the letter *G* with any color ink pad. Stamp *G* at center top of 1 cardstock page to the right of the perforation. Continue inking and stamping remaining letters to spell out GOOD FOR on page using the same color ink pad. Keep letters centered

toward the top of the page and leave room around the edges of the page. Let ink dry. Ink handprint stamp with the same color ink pad. Stamp handprint at lower right corner of page. Repeat with remaining inside pages using a different color ink for each page. Make sure you clean each stamp when you change colors.

3. Use remaining page to make coupon book cover. Starting with the letter *C*, ink alphabet stamp with any color ink pad. Stamp *C* on coupon book cover page to the right of the perforation near the top edge of page. Continue inking and stamping letters to spell out COUPON BOOK for MOM, keeping letters centered between the perforation and the right edge of page. Be sure to leave room around the edges of the page. Be creative and alternate colors. Just make sure

you clean each stamp when you change colors. Let ink dry. Ink handprint stamp with any color ink pad. Stamp on cover page at lower right corner.

4. Use the ruler and crayons to draw 4 lines each along the right edge and bottom edge of each page. Use a different color crayon for each line. Then have your child write on each inside page what that coupon can be redeemed for: taking out the trash, cleaning up his or her room, or walking the dog. For very young children, the coupons might be for a hug, a kiss, or a trip to the park.

5. Punch 2 holes toward the left edge of each page. Position the holes to the left of the perforation and about 1½-inches apart. Make sure holes are punched in the same position on each page. Gather all pages and bind together using a crayon and rubber band. Thread the rubber band up through the holes and wrap it around the crayon.

Black Facet Necklace

What a wonderful treasure to find in your stocking on Christmas morning! This dazzling beaded necklace looks elaborate yet is easy to make. It's the perfect complement to any special occasion outfit.

What You'll Need

3 gold bails, 7mm

3 black facet pendants, 9×32mm

6 gold eye pins, 2-inches long

4 gold jump rings, 6mm

85 black facet beads, 4mm

79 gold facet beads, 4mm

79 crystal facet beads, 4mm

1 black facet bicone bead,
16×18mm

10 black facet bicone beads,
10×13mm

20 gold flower spacers, 8mm

2 gold fluted endcaps,
⅞×½-inches

1 necklace clasp

64 inches waxed linen cord or
beading cord

Wire cutter

Round-nose pliers

Needle-nose pliers

Scissors

Craft glue

1. Attach bails to pendants. Insert bail ends into pendant holes and gently squeeze to secure.

2. Pendant Dangles: Use wire cutter to trim ¼-inch from end of 1 eye pin. Trim ½-inch from end of another eye pin. Use round-nose pliers to turn a small loop at the end of the 2 trimmed eye pins and at the end of 1 untrimmed eye pin. Use needle-nose pliers to open a jump ring. Slip bail of 1 pendant and eye of 1 eye pin on jump ring. Close jump ring with needle-nose pliers. Repeat with remaining 2 eye pins and pendants.

3. Beaded Eye Pin: Thread the following beads on an eye pin: 4mm black bead, flower spacer, 4mm black bead, 16×18mm bicone bead, 4mm black bead, flower spacer, and a 4mm black bead. Trim eye pin, leaving ¼-inch from end of last bead. Turn a small loop at end of eye pin. Loop should be snug against last bead.

4. Open a jump ring. Thread 3 pendant dangles and beaded eye pin on jump ring to form the necklace pendant. Close jump ring. Cut two 32-inch pieces of waxed linen cord. Thread both cord pieces through the eye of necklace pendant and center on cord. Set aside two 4mm black beads. Mix together the remaining 4mm black, crystal, and gold beads to use in a random pattern for the necklace.

5. Thread the following bead pattern on one half of necklace: On each strand of cord, string eleven 4mm beads. Then thread both strands through a flower spacer, a 10×13mm bicone bead, and another flower spacer. Repeat 3 more times. After bead pattern is complete, thread 14 more 4mm beads on each strand of cord. Thread both strands through a flower spacer and a 10×13mm bicone bead to complete one half of necklace.

6. Open the eye of 1 eye pin. Thread ends of both beaded strands (from completed half of necklace) through open eye and tie strand ends in a double knot. Secure knots with a dab of glue. Trim cord to about ⅛-inch from knots. Thread eye pin through a fluted endcap, making sure the bicone bead is snug against the wide end of endcap. Then thread a 4mm black bead on the eye pin. Trim eye pin, leaving ¼-inch from end of last bead. Turn a loop at end of eye pin. Do not close loop yet. Thread eye of one half of necklace clasp on loop before closing it completely. Close loop, making sure it is snug against last bead.

7. Repeat steps 5 and 6 for other half of necklace.

Pleated Tie-Dye Tshirt

Create a colorful T-shirt using a simple tie-dye technique. It makes a great stocking stuffer gift— just roll it up and tuck it in a Christmas stocking.

What You'll Need

White cotton T-shirt
Fabric dye: red, orange, yellow, green, blue, light blue, purple
6 rubber bands
Rubber gloves
7 squeeze bottles
Paper towels
Scissors

1. Soak shirt in bucket of cold water. Remove from water and wring water out. Lay shirt face down on work surface. Put left hand at tip of sleeve and other hand at bottom of shirt at corner. Fold over 2 inches.

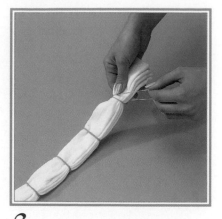

3. Wrap rubber band around center of folded shirt. Continue to wrap rubber bands around shirt every 2 inches (above and below center band). Use 6 rubber bands.

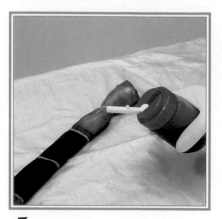

5. Turn T-shirt over and apply dye to the back side. Make sure to squeeze the same color dye in the same color section as on front. Continue until all sections are dyed.

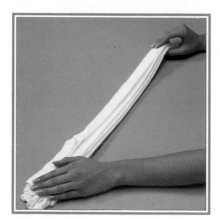

2. Flip shirt over onto back side and fold over 2 inches. Repeat folding every 2 inches and make sure to flip shirt over after each fold. (When finished, shirt should look like an accordion-pleated tube.)

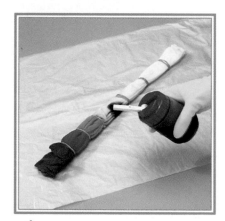

4. Wearing rubber gloves, prepare each color dye in a squeeze bottle. Start at the bottom of the shirt and squeeze red dye into the first rubber-banded section. Continue with the other sections. Apply dye in rainbow order (red, orange, yellow, green, blue, light blue, and purple).

6. Let dye set 30 to 60 minutes, then rinse under cold water and gently squeeze until water runs clear. Blot with paper towels. Cut rubber bands off with scissors. Unroll shirt and let air dry.

Fiesta Rose Trinket Box

*What better gift to give (and receive) than
this delicate rose-patterned trinket box.
This elegant keepsake will be treasured
for years to come.*

What You'll Need

6×6-inch piece 18- or 20-count
ivory cross-stitch cloth
Embroidery floss, 1 skein each
(see color key)
2×3-inch oval porcelain box
#24 tapestry needle
Scissors
Craft glue
Pencil

Instructions: Cross stitch using 2 strands of floss. Stitch according to the chart.

To finish: When cross-stitch is complete, trim excess fabric. Place cross-stitching face up on a flat surface. Remove all parts from lid of porcelain box. Position the gold rim of lid around cross-stitching so that the design is centered in the open area. Trace around the outside edge of the lid. Cut fabric following traced line.

To assemble lid: Place the clear acetate in the gold rim. Place cross-stitched piece with design face down on acetate. Position the sponge over the design. Then push the metal locking disk firmly in place. If a flocked lid liner is included, add a few drops of glue to secure it in place over the metal disk.

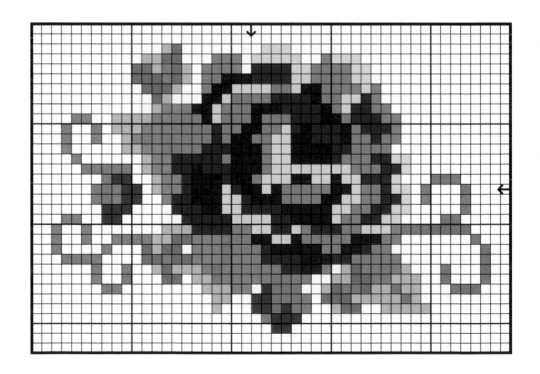

3803 Burgundy
3687 Red
3354 Dark Pink
963 Light Pink
3815 Dark Green
3816 Light Green
3013 Olive Green
799 Dark Blue
800 Light Blue
208 Purple
210 Lavender

Victorian Picture Frame

Add a touch of romance to Christmas with a heart-shaped picture frame. The elegant velvet fabric and decorative brass charms provide the delicate Victorian look of this charming frame.

What You'll Need

¼ yard burgundy velvet fabric
¼ yard burgundy fabric
⅓ yard iron-on fabric adhesive
Posterboard or cardboard
5–6 assorted heart charms
12 inches white ribbon,
⅛-inch wide
3 white ribbon roses
Tracing paper
Pencil
Scissors
Iron
Hot glue gun and glue sticks

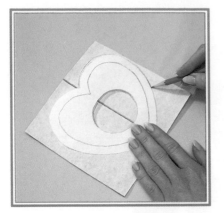

1. Iron fabric adhesive to back of velvet fabric and burgundy fabric. Trace 1 heart frame front pattern on tracing paper. Cut out pattern leaving a ⅜-inch allowance along inside and outside edges. Trace heart pattern on paper backing of velvet fabric. Trace 2 heart frame backs and 2 frame stand patterns on paper backing of burgundy fabric. Leave a ⅜-inch allowance along outside edge of 1 frame back piece and 1 frame stand piece. Cut out all traced pieces.

2. Trace 1 heart frame front pattern, 1 heart frame back pattern, and 1 frame stand pattern on posterboard. Cut out all traced pieces.

3. Remove paper backing from velvet fabric piece. Center posterboard heart frame front on back of velvet fabric piece. Iron in place, being careful not to touch exposed adhesive on velvet fabric with iron. Clip excess fabric around inside and outside edges in Vs, making sure not to clip too close to posterboard. Use iron to press clipped edges to posterboard.

4. Remove paper backing from burgundy fabric piece with ⅜-inch material allowance. Center posterboard heart frame back on back of burgundy fabric piece. Iron in place, being careful not to touch exposed adhesive on fabric with iron. Clip excess fabric around outside edge in Vs ¼-inch apart,

making sure not to clip too close to posterboard. Use iron to press clipped edge to posterboard. Remove paper backing from second burgundy fabric piece. Place fabric piece on back of posterboard heart and iron in place.

5. Remove paper backing from fabric stand piece with ⅜-inch material allowance. Center posterboard stand piece on back of fabric piece. Iron in place, being careful not to touch exposed adhesive on fabric with iron. Clip corners of fabric, making sure not to clip too close to posterboard. Fold edges over and iron in place. Remove paper backing from second fabric stand piece. Place fabric piece on back of posterboard stand and iron in place. Fold stand about ½-inch from top edge.

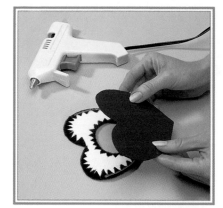

6. Apply a thin line of glue to back of frame front piece along sides and bottom. Place frame back piece over glue on front piece, keeping ends even. Leave top of frame unglued to add photo. Glue stand to back of frame.

7. Following finished project photo, glue assorted heart charms and ribbon roses to front of frame. Tie white ribbon in a bow and glue bow to front of frame. Loop ribbon ends around ribbon roses and charms and glue in place.

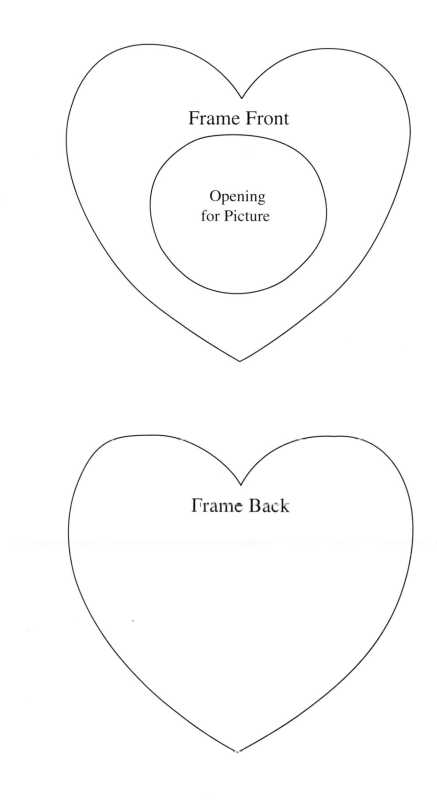

Frame Front

Opening
for Picture

Frame Back

Fold

Picture
Stand

Enlarge at 125%

Sticker Fun School Supply Box

Surprise your child with a fun school supply box. It's so easy to make—just paint a cigar-style box and then decorate it with your child's favorite stickers.

What You'll Need

Cigar-style school box
2–3 sheets of children's stickers
Holly berry red acrylic paint
Decoupage sealer
Acrylic sealer
2 foam brushes, 1-inch and
2¾-inch
Scissors

1. Basecoat entire school box with red paint using 2¾-inch foam brush. Allow to dry. Paint a second coat if necessary. Make sure paint has dried completely between coats.

2. Cut out desired shapes from 1 sticker sheet. Be creative and use as much design from the sheet as possible. Do not remove paper backing from stickers. Position stickers on top of box to create scene. When "picture" is formed, carefully remove paper backing from stickers and press in place on box top. Cut additional stickers from remaining sheets, remove paper backings, and press stickers on inside of lid and sides of box in a random pattern.

3. Apply a coat of decoupage sealer to finished school supply box using 1-inch foam brush. Allow to dry completely and apply a second coat if desired. Finish with 2 or 3 light coats of acrylic sealer, allowing sufficient drying time between coats.

Teacher's Pencil Holder

Stumped for something special for a #1 teacher? This personalized pencil holder is the perfect present on its own or in a teacher's gift stocking. Add pencils, erasers, magnets, and the Teacher's Crayon Box Pin on page 38 for more stocking stuffers.

What You'll Need

1 plastic organizer
Alphabet stamp set
Crayon stamp
Ink pads: yellow, blue, green, red, purple
Scrap paper
Green spray paint *(optional)*
Newspapers

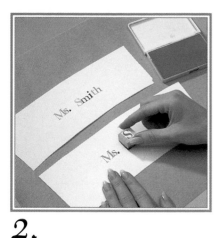

2.

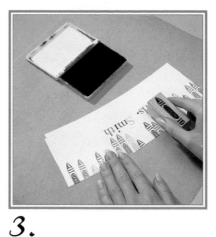

3.

4.

1. If desired, paint lid of organizer. Remove lid from organizer. Spread newspapers on work surface in a well-ventilated area. Spray 2 or 3 light coats of green paint on lid. Let paint dry completely between coats. Set lid aside.

2. Remove liner from organizer. Set aside. Pick out the alphabet stamps you need to spell out the teacher's name. Ink an alphabet stamp with any color ink pad and stamp on a scrap piece of paper. Continue inking and stamping teacher's name on scrap paper to plan placement and spacing of letters. Adjust as needed. Ink and stamp the name in the middle of liner using assorted ink colors. Be sure to clean stamps when you change colors.

3. Ink crayon stamp with yellow ink pad. Stamp along top edge and bottom edge of liner, repeating wherever you want a yellow crayon to appear. Clean the stamp. Continue inking and stamping with remaining colors, progressing from the lightest to darkest color (purple). Be sure to clean the stamp between colors and let ink dry.

4. Let ink dry thoroughly and insert liner. Place lid on organizer.

Teacher's Crayon Box Pin

You'll get an "A" for awesome when you make this creative crayon box pin for your favorite teacher. Cut out crayon shapes from foam and decorate with colorful ribbon for a quick and easy stocking stuffer gift.

What You'll Need

6 foam sheets: red, orange, yellow, green, blue, purple

Shiny black fabric paint

5 inches green ribbon, 1-inch wide

10 inches crayon print ribbon, ⅞-inch wide

2 × 2-inch piece cardboard

Bar pin, 1¼-inch long

Scissors

Pen or marker

Ruler

Hot glue gun and glue sticks

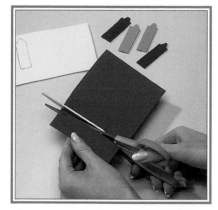

1. Trace crayon pattern on foam. Trace 1 each on orange, yellow, green, purple, and blue foam. Trace 2 on red foam. Cut crayon pieces from foam.

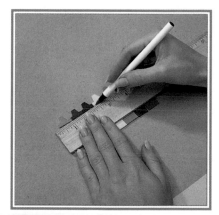

2. Line up all 7 crayon pieces in a row. Place a ruler across the row of crayons. Draw 2 lines across the top of each crayon. Be sure to keep crayons in a straight line. This helps to keep the lines even on each crayon. Draw a 5/16-inch-wide oval on the center of each crayon.

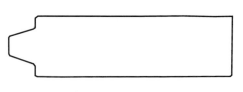

Enlarge at 125%

3. Take bottle of black fabric paint and gently squeeze paint along drawn lines at top of each crayon. Allow to dry. Then fill in the oval on each crayon with black paint. Let dry.

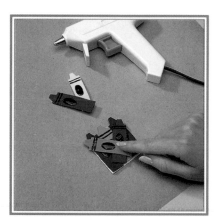

4. Glue purple, green, and blue crayons onto 2×2-inch piece of cardboard. Glue 1 red crayon diagonally across purple, green, and blue crayons with tip of red crayon at top right side of blue crayon. Glue orange crayon on top of red crayon at a diagonal in the opposite direction. Glue yellow crayon on top of red crayon (over base of orange crayon) in a vertical position, being careful not to cover tip of blue crayon. Glue second red crayon to center of glued crayons at a slight

diagonal toward the left. Trim bottom ends of crayons if they extend beyond cardboard.

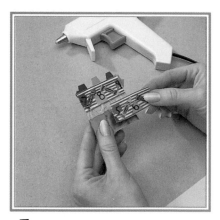

5. Glue a 5-inch piece of green ribbon along bottom edge of cardboard, covering crayon ends. Glue ends of ribbon to back of cardboard. Cut two 2-inch pieces of crayon print ribbon. Glue ribbon pieces to back of cardboard with 1 piece at the top and 1 piece in the center. Glue bar pin to back of covered cardboard.

6. To form bow, cut a 5-inch piece of crayon print ribbon. Glue ends together to form a loop. Cut a 1-inch piece of crayon print ribbon for center tie piece. Place a dab of glue down center back of 1-inch ribbon piece. Fold ribbon piece in thirds. Pinch ribbon loop together at center and wrap center tie piece around it. Glue in place. Glue bow to front of crayon box pin.

Terrific Tote Bag

How do you make a useful yet attractive gift your kids will like? Make an ordinary tote bag extraordinary with webbing spray and paint. The webbing spray creates a marbleized look while the black paint adds dimension.

What You'll Need

Medium-size tote bag
Webbing spray: black lava,
teal lattice, plum punch
Shiny black fabric paint
18-inch ruler
Disappearing ink pen
Craft paper or plastic garbage bag
(to cover work surface)

40

1.

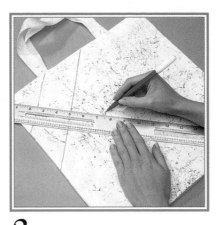

2.

3.

1. Cover work surface with craft paper or plastic garbage bag. Lay tote bag flat on work surface. Shake can of black lava webbing spray and hold it 10 to 12 inches from bag. Spray bag with webbing spray, moving your hand quickly across the surface as you spray. Repeat with teal lattice and then plum punch webbing spray. Let dry. Turn tote bag over and spray webbing on back side. Make sure to spray bottom gusset of tote bag. Let dry.

2. Use ruler to measure from top left corner of bag to bottom right corner. Use disappearing ink pen to mark points at 2½ inches, 5 inches, 7½ inches, 10 inches, 12½ inches, and 15 inches. Draw a diagonal line across tote bag at each measured point.

3. Using bottle of black fabric paint, squeeze paint along drawn lines. Paint dots, zig-zags, straight lines, or other designs following the lines on the tote bag. Let paint dry.

4. Repeat steps 2 and 3 for other side of tote bag. (Note: Tote bag is machine washable. Wash bag on gentle cycle as needed.)

Keepsake Key Chains

Make a key chain for the music lover, baseball fanatic, or chocoholic in your life. They'll appreciate a painted wood key chain made just for them.

What You'll Need

(for each key chain)

Wood disk with key chain, 3-inch diameter

Tracing paper

Transfer paper

Pencil

Paintbrushes: ½-inch and #2 flat, 10/0 liner

⅜-inch angle paint brush (for Baseball Lovers and Chocolate Lovers)

Stylus

Matte finish spray

Acrylic paints for:

Music Lovers:
snow white, cadmium red, ebony black

Baseball Lovers:
snow white, french grey-blue, cadmium red, ebony black

Chocolate Lovers:
buttermilk, sable brown, dark chocolate, ebony black

Music Lovers Key Chain

1. Remove chain from disk. Use ½-inch flat brush to basecoat entire wood disk with white paint. Let dry.

2. Transfer pattern to painted wood disk (see step 2 of Cook's Plaque on page 60). When you apply the notes to the disk, apply only the dots of the notes for placement. Do not apply the stem of the notes. Use #2 flat brush to paint heart with cadmium red. Let dry. Dab stylus with black paint and dot notes on disk following pattern. Line *I*, treble clef, and notes with black paint. Outline red heart with black paint. Once paint is dry, spray key chain with a matte finish.

3. Repeat step 2 for other side of key chain. Attach chain.

To make the other key chains, follow the same procedures described in steps 1 through 3 using appropriate paints and patterns. See finished project photo for paint placement. To float a shade of paint, see page 8.

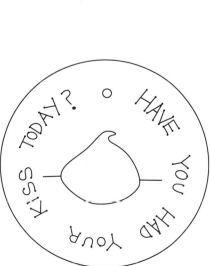

Enlarge at 150%

Funky Friendship Bracelet

Beaded friendship bracelets are fun and easy
to make. Your kids can give their friends
a truly special stocking stuffer gift they made
themselves. The unique memory wire makes the
bracelet adjustable to fit any size wrist.

What You'll Need

1 bracelet memory wire
Round letter beads, 6mm
(to spell out desired name)
14 round heart beads, 6mm
2 silver heart charms
90–120 red glass seed beads,
size E
Round-nose pliers
Needle-nose pliers
Wire cutter

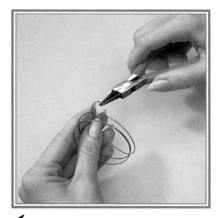

1.

2.

1. Use round-nose pliers to turn a loop at one end of bracelet wire. The wire may be difficult to bend; bend loop as far as you can without completely closing it. Slide 1 heart charm on end loop. Close loop by squeezing it together with needle-nose pliers.

2. Line up the letter beads to see how long the name will be. The name will be approximately centered on the bracelet wire. You can estimate where to begin threading the letter beads as you work. Thread bead pattern onto bracelet wire as follows: 7 red seed beads and 1 heart bead. Push beads against looped end as you work. Repeat bead pattern until the beads reach the middle of wire minus half the length of the name. Thread letter beads on wire to spell out the name. Then continue threading the bead pattern to mirror the order on the other side of the name.

3. Trim bracelet wire end if necessary. Turn a loop at the end of the wire. Do not close loop. Insert remaining heart charm before closing the loop completely.

Tic-Tac-Toe Game

Hugs and kisses will abound when your child looks in his or her stocking and finds this colorful tic-tac-toe game. Boy and girl wood pieces make up the X's and O's—a muslin bag keeps all the pieces conveniently together.

1.

2.

3.

What You'll Need

5 boy wood cutouts

5 girl wood cutouts

Acrylic paints: flesh, bright yellow, orange, black, burnt sienna, pink, copen blue, green

Permanent markers: red and black

Green fabric paint

Muslin bag

Paintbrush

Stylus

Waxed paper

Ruler

Disappearing ink pen

1. Paint bodies of girl cutouts yellow. Paint bodies of boy cutouts orange. Be sure to paint back side of bodies and all around the edges. Let dry. Paint faces using flesh. Use stylus to dot flesh for hands. Add black dots with stylus to boy cutouts for feet. Allow paint to dry. Draw *X*'s on boy cutouts and *O*'s on girl cutouts using black marker.

2. Use stylus to dot blue eyes on boy cutouts and green eyes on girl cutouts. Let dry. Dot burnt sienna freckles on boys. Dot pink cheeks for girls. Allow to dry. Draw a smile on each face using red marker.

3. Place a sheet of waxed paper in muslin bag. Use a ruler and disappearing ink pen to draw tic-tac-toe lines on front of muslin bag. Using bottle of green fabric paint, squeeze paint along lines. Allow to dry and remove waxed paper. Place finished boy and girl tic-tac-toe pieces in bag.

Starstruck Photo Album

Styles may come and go, but photos last forever. A photo album painted in funky colors makes a great gift for that hard to buy for teen.

What You'll Need

Canvas covered photo book
Acrylic paints: ebony black,
purple pearl metallic,
turquoise pearl metallic,
glorious gold metallic
Matte finish spray
2 flat paintbrushes: ½-inch and #2
Tracing paper
Transfer paper
Pencil
Paper bag

2.

3.

1. Basecoat front and back covers of photo album with purple pearl using ½-inch flat brush. Let dry.

2. Transfer pattern to photo album cover (see step 2 of Cook's Plaque on page 60). Using #2 flat brush, paint wavy line and coiled line with black, paint star with gold, and paint straight lines with turquoise pearl. Let dry.

3. Dilute black paint with water. Practice splattering paint with ½-inch flat brush on a paper bag until desired consistency is achieved. Lightly splatter photo album cover with paint. Let dry.

4. Repeat steps 2 and 3 on reverse side of photo album. Spray with matte finish.

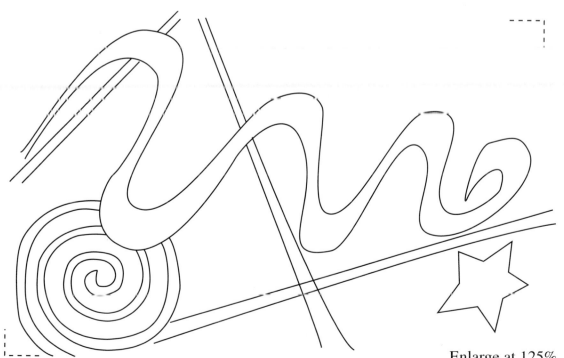

Enlarge at 125%

Book Lover's Bookmarks

Books are for people of all ages and interests—every reader needs a special bookmark. Choose one of these creative designs to put in a book lover's stocking.

What You'll Need

(for each bookmark)
2½ × 12½-inch piece background fabric
2–3 pieces fabric scraps
(for appliques)
½ yard iron-on fabric adhesive
2½ × 12½-inch piece iron-on flexible vinyl
6-inch piece yarn or 3-inch tassel
Charm or beads
(for end of yarn piece)
Tracing or typing paper
Pen or pencil
Scissors
Iron
Fine point black fabric marker
(for fish bookmark)
Craft knife
Ruler
Hole punch

Fish Bookmark

1. Iron adhesive to back of 2 applique fabric pieces. Trace fish pattern to back of 1 fabric piece. Draw "gills" on second piece. Cut out pieces and remove paper backing. Center fish applique about ½-inch from bottom edge and each side of background fabric piece and iron in place. Place "gills" on fish and iron in place. Use black fabric marker to draw eye on fish and water bubbles on background fabric.

2. Cut a 2½×6¼-inch piece of fabric adhesive. Place adhesive strip on back of background fabric at opposite end of appliques, keeping edges even. Iron adhesive in place. Do not remove paper backing.

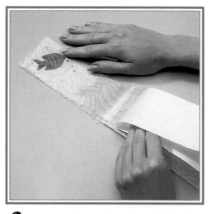

3. Place bookmark flat on work surface with right side up. Take flexible vinyl piece and slowly peel paper backing about 2 to 3 inches down from vinyl. Place sticky side of vinyl down at one end of bookmark. Peel paper backing from vinyl as you press vinyl in place on bookmark, keeping edges even. Place paper backing, shiny side down, over vinyl and press with iron for 3 to 4 seconds. Remove paper and allow to cool.

4. Turn bookmark over and remove paper backing. Fold bookmark in half over the paper backing. Place paper backing piece from step 3 over the folded bookmark. Press with iron for 1 to 2 seconds to fuse front and back together.

5. Measure and mark ¼-inch from applique to bottom and side edges of bookmark. Use a craft knife to trim bookmark to 2×6-inches. Punch a hole at center of top of bookmark ¼-inch from the edge. Thread a charm through 6-inch yarn piece and knot ends together. Insert one end of yarn loop through punched bookmark hole. Slip end of yarn with charm through the loop and pull to tighten. Trim ends.

To make other bookmarks, follow the same procedures described in steps 1 through 5 using appropriate patterns.

Enlarge at 200%

Sunflower Coasters

Create a gift that's used year round.
Cheerful sunflowers stitched on plastic canvas
will brighten up any home all
through the year.

What You'll Need

(to make 1 coaster)
1 sheet clear plastic canvas,
10 count
Embroidery floss, 1 skein each
(see color key)
#20 tapestry needle
Scissors
4×4-inch piece gold or rust felt
Craft glue

Instructions: Cut a plastic
canvas square 40×40-holes.

Stitching: Stitch design
following the chart. Work
design in continental stitch,
using 12 strands of floss
(double the length of floss).
Overcast all edges in ivory.
Use 12 strands of floss for
overcasting.

To Finish: Apply a thin line of
glue around the outer edges of
4×4-inch felt piece. Apply a
few dots of glue at center of
felt. Place stitched piece on felt
over the glue. Hold and press
gently until glue around the
edges begins to dry.

■	469	Dark Green
■	471	Light Green
■	834	Olive Gold
■	743	Pale Yellow
■	972	Medium Yellow
■	977	Gold
■	922	Light Brown
■	920	Dark Brown
■	712	Ivory

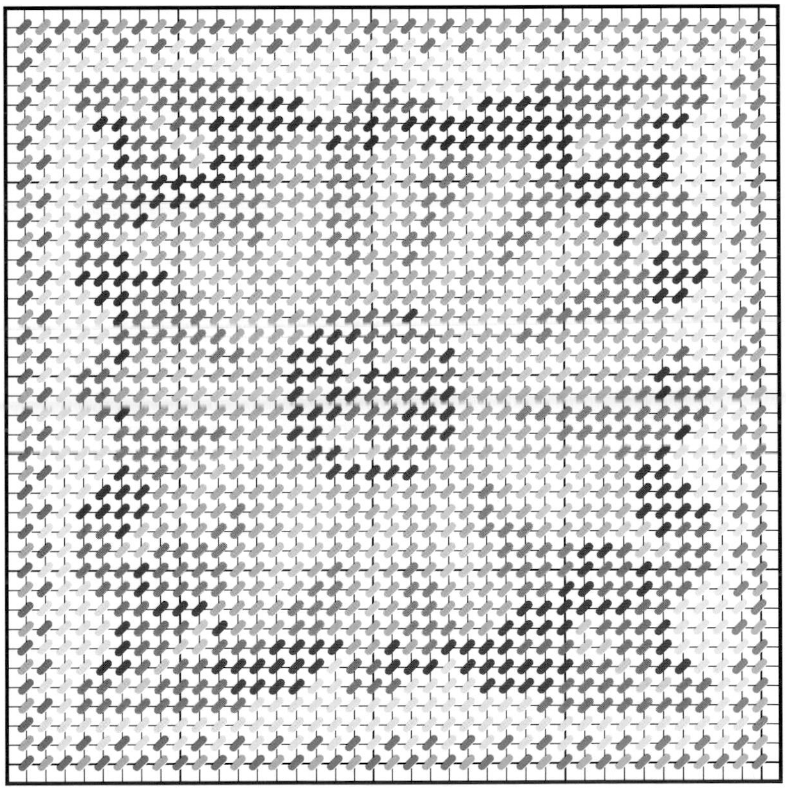

Fabric Picture Frame

What a great way to display and enjoy a favorite photo. This lightly padded 5×7-inch frame is perfect for the desk or mantle and can hold a 4×6-inch photo. A picture frame made with love is an ideal stocking stuffer gift for a special person.

What You'll Need

¼ yard background fabric *(solid, pindot, or tone-on-tone)*

¼ yard fabric with a 1-inch-wide stripe design

¼ yard iron-on fabric adhesive

1¼ yard iron-on fusible adhesive, ⅜-inch-wide roll

7 × 10-inch piece cardboard

¼ yard batting or craft fleece

Tracing paper

Pen or pencil

Scissors

Iron

Craft knife

Glue stick

Ruler with 45 degree angle marking

1. Trace frame pattern on cardboard. Trace around inside and outside edges of pattern for frame front piece and trace around outside edges for frame back piece. Trace stand pattern on cardboard in the inside area of the frame front. Use a craft knife to cut out all traced pieces. Fold stand about ½-inch from top edge.

2. Trace frame pattern on back of background fabric. Cut frame front fabric piece, leaving a ¾-inch material allowance along the inside and outside edges. Iron pieces of ⅜-inch-wide adhesive to the back of inside and outside edges of frame front fabric piece. Do not remove paper backing. Cut the inner corner points to the traced line of inside edge.

3. Iron a 9 × 12-inch piece of adhesive to back of remaining background fabric piece. Trace frame pattern on paper backing. Trace around outside edge of pattern for 1 frame back piece. Repeat for a second back piece. Trace stand pattern on paper backing. Turn pattern piece to the reverse side and trace again for second stand piece. Cut all pieces and remove paper backing. Iron fabric back pieces to both sides of cardboard frame back piece. Iron fabric stand pieces to both sides of cardboard stand piece.

4. Place stand on frame back piece with the point at one corner and the bottom edge straight along the frame bottom. Glue folded top edge of stand in place.

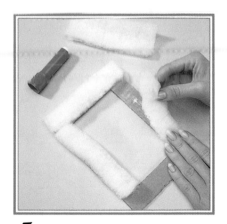

5. Cut four 2 × 5-inch pieces of batting. Fold each piece in half lengthwise and glue edges together. Glue batting pieces to cardboard frame front.

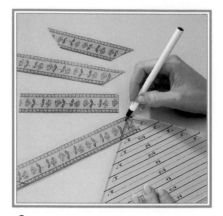

6. Cut remaining adhesive into four 1¼×9-inch strips. Center and iron each strip on back of fabric with 1-inch-wide strip design. Cut the 4 strips along the printed design line and remove paper backing. Trim 2 strips to 7 inches and 2 strips to 5 inches. Using the 45 degree angle line on the ruler, mark a right triangle from both ends of each strip. Cut along marks, making each strip into a trapezoid. Center strips on frame front fabric piece from step 2, matching corners of trapezoids. Iron in place. Remove paper backing from the ⅜-inch adhesive strips on back of frame fabric.

7. Place the frame front fabric piece over the batting-

covered cardboard frame front piece. Trim off a triangular piece from each outer corner of fabric. Fold fabric edges over to the cardboard back and iron in place.

8. Apply a thin line of glue to back of frame front piece along sides and bottom, leaving the top edge open to insert the photo. Place frame back piece over glue on front piece, keeping ends even.

Frame

Stand   Fold

Enlarge at 125%

Veggie Magnets & Memo Holder

These clay refrigerator magnets bring together the fine detail of rubber stamps and the sturdiness of polymer clay to create little pieces of kitchen art. The memo holder is terrific for holding recipes or a shopping list.

What You'll Need

2 packages polymer clay, white
Waxed paper
Veggie stamps: Indian corn, lettuce, green beans, carrots, radishes
Pigment ink pad, black
Aluminum foil
Facial tissues
Ultra-soft colored pencils: yellow, gold, orange, burnt orange, dark red, green, light green, dark green
Water-based varnish, clear
10-inch piece magnetic strip
White acrylic paint
Wood clothespin
Rolling pin
Craft knife *(#11 blade)*
Baking sheet
Emery board
Cotton swabs
Small foam brush
Flat paintbrush
Scissors
Craft glue

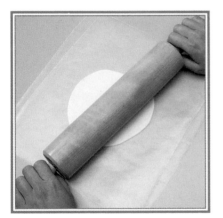

1. Knead a 3-inch ball of polymer clay until soft, then on the waxed paper roll it out with the rolling pin to ⅛-inch thickness. Carefully lift and turn over so the clay doesn't stick to the waxed paper. Repeat with a second 3-inch ball of clay.

2. Ink the lettuce stamp with the black pigment ink and press into clay. Repeat with green beans, carrots, radishes, and Indian corn stamps.

3. Using the craft knife, cut out each image as close as possible to the inked line. Avoid pulling the clay or cutting through the waxed paper. After all images are cut out, transfer them to a baking sheet lined with aluminum foil. Avoid smearing the ink or stretching the clay. Lay facial tissues over the images and press gently to blot excess ink.

4. Bake 15 to 20 minutes at 250 degrees F. Let cool before handling. If needed, smooth the edges with an emery board.

5. Color the lettuce light green, the green beans dark green, the carrots burnt orange with green leaves, and the radishes dark red with green leaves. Color the Indian corn husks gold and the rope tie green. Go over the corn kernels with yellow, gold, orange, and dark red pencils. Use cotton swabs to blend colors on vegetables.

6. With the small foam brush, apply a thin coat of varnish to the front of each piece. Let dry. Repeat for the edges and back of each piece. Add more varnish to the fronts for higher gloss, letting dry between coats.

7. Use the flat paintbrush to apply white paint to the clothespin. Let dry. Apply a second coat if necessary.

8. Cut a piece of magnetic strip to fit lettuce, green beans, carrots, and radishes. Cut a 3½-inch piece of magnetic strip for Indian corn. Glue 3½-inch magnet piece to one side of the painted clothespin and glue the Indian corn to the other side. Glue remaining magnet pieces to back of each clay piece.

Cook's Plaque

Warm the heart of your favorite cook with a gift stocking filled with goodies. Add this painted plaque, the oven mitt and pot holder set on page 61, the veggie magnets on page 57, and other items such as herbs and spices, recipe cards, and wood utensils.

What You'll Need

Wood and wire hanging sign kit

Acrylic paints: buttermilk, amish blue, heartland blue, neutral grey, metallic silver, black, cadmium red, tan, dark chocolate

Paintbrushes: ½-inch and #2 flat, ⅜-inch angle, 10/0 liner

Scrap of country print fabric

Tracing paper

Transfer paper

Pencil

Craft glue

Matte finish spray

1. Use ½-inch flat brush to basecoat entire plaque with buttermilk and let dry.

2. Trace pattern on tracing paper. Place a piece of transfer paper, carbon side down, on painted wood plaque. Place traced pattern on wood plaque over the transfer paper, and tape in place to hold. To transfer pattern, use a pencil to trace over the lines of the pattern. Remove tape and papers from plaque.

3. Use #2 flat brush to paint heart cadmium red, COOKING amish blue, and spoon tan. Line whisk with neutral grey. Allow paint to dry. Set heart aside.

4. Dilute buttermilk paint with water. Following pattern in photo, paint fabric pattern on COOKING using diluted buttermilk. Let dry.

5. Float a shade on COOKING letters using heartland blue and ⅜-inch angle brush (see page 8). Float a shade on spoon using dark chocolate. Highlight whisk with lines of metallic silver. Once paint is dry, line COOKING letters with black. Paint WARMS THE with black and 10/0 liner.

6. Once paint is dry, glue heart in place. Spray plaque with a matte finish and let dry. Attach wire hanger to plaque. Tie a piece of scrap fabric around wire to finish.

Enlarge at 125%

Country Kitchen Oven Mitt & Pot Holder Set

Use an applique motif from your favorite print fabric to decorate a pot holder and oven mitt. Pretty and practical, they can be made to match any kitchen decor.

What You'll Need

(for oven mitt)
¼ yard navy blue quilted fabric
¼ yard kitchen print fabric
(for applique)
½ yard navy print ribbon,
⅝-inch wide
¼ yard iron-on fabric adhesive
12 inches iron-on fabric adhesive,
⅝-inch-wide roll

(for pot holder)
¼ yard red quilted fabric
¼ yard kitchen print fabric
(for applique)
1 yard navy print ribbon,
⅝-inch wide
¼ yard iron-on fabric adhesive
1 yard iron-on fabric adhesive,
⅝-inch-wide roll

(for both)
Pencil
Scissors
Straight pins
Iron
Sewing machine
White thread
Sewing needle
Ruler

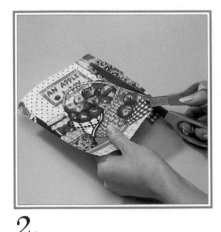

2.

3.

4.

5.

6.

1. Fold quilted fabric in half with right sides together. Trace oven mitt pattern. Pin pattern piece to folded fabric and cut 2 mitt pieces.

2. Iron adhesive to back of kitchen print fabric. Cut out a 3- to 4-inch applique design. Remove paper backing. Center applique design on front of 1 mitt piece. Iron in place.

3. Set the sewing machine for medium width zig-zag stitch. Sew around the edge of the applique to secure.

4. Cut a 12-inch piece of ribbon. Iron the ⅝-inch-wide adhesive strip to back of ribbon. Remove paper backing. Cut ribbon in two 6-inch pieces. Fold the ribbon in half lengthwise and encase the bottom edge of each mitt piece, pinning in place to secure. Iron ribbon in place. Remove pins. Straight stitch along the ribbon edge to secure.

5. Cut a 3-inch piece from remaining ribbon. Fold ribbon in half lengthwise and stitch the edges together. Bring ribbon ends together to form a loop. Stitch ribbon loop to inside top of back mitt piece ¼-inch from the side edge.

6. Pin mitt piece together with back sides facing out. Zig-zag stitch the 2 mitt pieces together around the entire edge, removing pins as you go along. Turn mitt right side out.

Pot Holder

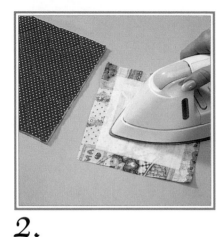

2.

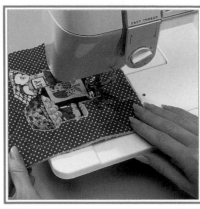

3.

4.

5.

6.

1. Cut two 7-inch squares of quilted fabric for front and back of pot holder.

2. Iron adhesive to back of kitchen print fabric. Cut out a 3- to 4-inch applique design. Remove paper backing. Center applique design on front of 1 square pot holder piece. Iron in place.

3. Set the sewing machine for medium width zig-zag stitch. Sew around the edge of the applique to secure.

4. Cut four 7-inch pieces of ribbon. Cut four 7-inch pieces of ⅝-inch-wide adhesive. Iron 7-inch adhesive strips to back of 7-inch ribbon pieces. Remove paper backing. Pin 2 pot holder pieces together with right sides facing out.

5. Fold a piece of ribbon in half lengthwise and encase the top edge of pot holder, pinning in place to secure. Iron ribbon in place. Remove pins. Repeat for the bottom edge of pot holder, removing pins as you go along. Straight stitch along the top and bottom ribbon edges to secure.

6. Cut a 3-inch piece from remaining ribbon. Fold ribbon in half lengthwise and stitch the edges together. Bring ribbon ends together to form a loop. Stitch ribbon loop to top left back of pot holder.

7. Follow step 5 to bind the remaining 2 sides of pot holder.

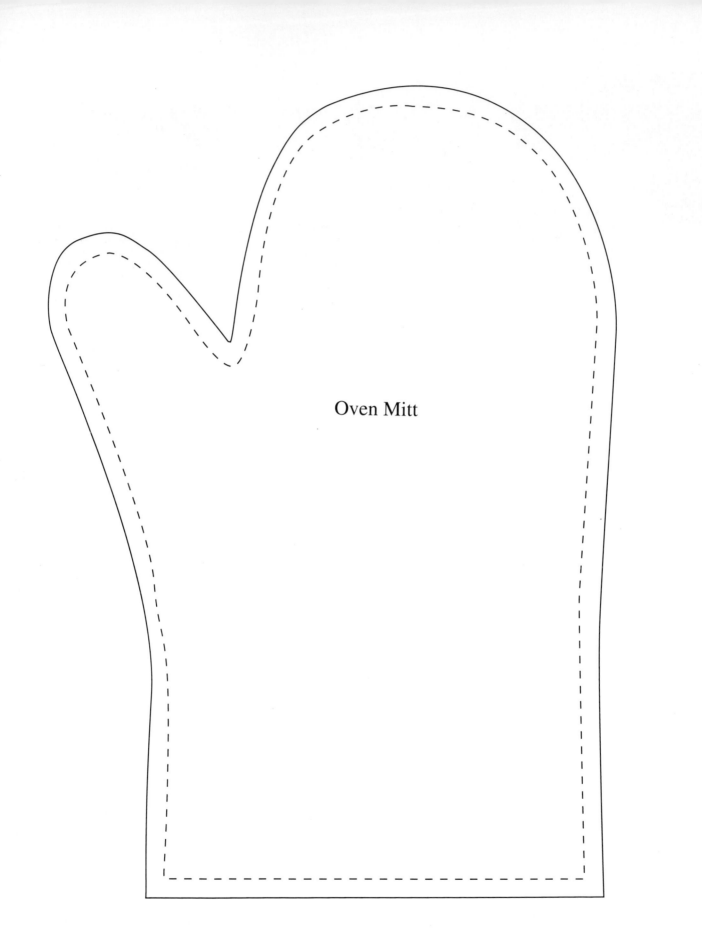

Oven Mitt

Enlarge at 125%